Saving Dogs in Ameirca: A Journey of Compassion, Advocacy, and Resilience in the Canine Rescue Movement

Randy Woodrum

Published by Randy Woodrum, 2024.

While every precaution has been taken in the preparation of this book, the publisher assumes no responsibility for errors or omissions, or for damages resulting from the use of the information contained herein.

SAVING DOGS IN AMEIRCA: A JOURNEY OF COMPASSION, ADVOCACY, AND RESILIENCE IN THE CANINE RESCUE MOVEMENT

First edition. January 21, 2024.

Copyright © 2024 Randy Woodrum.

ISBN: 979-8224763474

Written by Randy Woodrum.

Chapter 1: The Predicament of Rescue Dogs in America

The Overpopulation Crisis

In recent years, the United States has been facing an alarming crisis that is affecting our beloved pets: overpopulation. This crisis has reached such levels that it poses a significant challenge to the welfare and survival of rescue dogs across the country. This book will explore the causes, consequences, and possible solutions to this pressing issue. One of the primary causes of the overpopulation crisis is the lack of responsible pet ownership. Many individuals fail to spay or neuter their pets, allowing them to reproduce unchecked. This results in an exponential increase in the number of stray and unwanted dogs, placing an enormous burden on animal shelters and rescue organizations. Additionally, some pet owners irresponsibly abandon their furry companions, further exacerbating the problem. According to the American Society for the Prevention of Cruelty to Animals (ASPCA), approximately 6.5 million companion animals enter U.S. animal shelters nationwide each year. This data includes both dogs and cats.

The consequences of overpopulation are devastating. Shelters become overcrowded, leading to limited resources, insufficient space, and compromised living conditions for the animals. As a result, countless rescue dogs are euthanized each year due to the sheer volume of animals and limited adoption opportunities. This heartbreaking reality highlights the urgent need for action. While the number of euthanized animals has decreased over the years, it is still a concern. In recent years, the euthanasia rate for dogs has been around 670,000 annually based on reported data. However, it's essential to note that this number has significantly decreased compared to previous decades.

To combat the overpopulation crisis, it is imperative that pet owners take responsibility for their pets. Spaying or neutering is a simple, effective, and humane solution that can prevent countless unwanted litter. Educational campaigns should also be implemented to raise awareness about the importance of responsible pet ownership and the benefits of adoption. The success of spaying and neutering campaigns has contributed to reducing the number of unwanted litter and, subsequently, the population of dogs in shelters.

By fostering a culture of compassion and empathy towards animals, we can encourage more individuals to adopt rescue dogs instead of purchasing from breeders. Supporting local animal shelters and rescue organizations through donations, volunteering, or fostering can also make a significant difference in the lives of these animals. The adoption rates for dogs have been positive, with millions finding loving homes each year. According to the ASPCA, around 3.3 million dogs enter U.S. animal shelters annually, and about 3.2 million are adopted. The government must also step up and enact legislation to regulate breeders and pet stores, ensuring they operate ethically and responsibly. Stricter penalties for animal abandonment and abuse should be implemented to deter such cruel actions. Furthermore, government-funded initiatives can provide financial support for low-income individuals to spay or neuter their pets, reducing the number of unwanted litters.

The overpopulation crisis is a pressing issue that demands immediate attention from pet owners, society, and the government. By promoting responsible pet ownership, raising awareness, supporting rescue organizations, and enacting legislation, we can work together to alleviate the suffering of rescue dogs in America. Let us unite our voices and advocate for change, becoming the voice for the voiceless.

The Struggles of Shelter Life

Shelter life is far from ideal for dogs who have already endured traumatic experiences. The loud noises, confined spaces, and lack of personal attention can contribute to anxiety, fear, and behavioral issues. Many rescue dogs suffer from separation anxiety, making their time in a shelter even more distressing. It is crucial for pet owners to understand that these struggles can significantly impact a dog's overall well-being and future adoption prospects.

Life within the confines of a shelter presents a myriad of challenges for dogs, transforming what should be a haven into a temporary refuge marked by uncertainty. The most palpable struggle is the pervasive sense of confinement; once accustomed to the boundless outdoors or the warmth of a family home, these dogs find themselves confined to small kennels, their world reduced to concrete floors and chain-link fences. These cacophony of barks, whimpers, and the ever-present scent of unfamiliar companions creates a sensory overload, amplifying stress and anxiety. Shelter dogs often endure a profound sense of abandonment, left yearning for the human connection they once knew.

For those who have faced neglect or mistreatment, the scars of their past linger, manifesting as behavioral issues that further complicate their path to adoption. The constant exposure to the unknown and the lack of a stable routine exacerbate their anxiety, making the shelter environment a challenging place for them to express their true selves. Overcrowded conditions and limited resources amplify the struggle, with each dog vying for attention and a chance to stand out among the multitude.

Despite the best efforts of dedicated shelter staff and volunteers, the sheer volume of dogs in need can make it difficult to provide individualized care. In the face of these challenges, however, dogs exhibit an incredible resilience, showcasing a remarkable ability to adapt and, with the right support, overcome the struggles of shelter life to find a second chance at love and companionship. By raising awareness, we hope to break the stereotypes associated with shelter dogs and provide them with the compassion they deserve. These dogs are not "damaged goods" or "problematic cases" but rather resilient beings who need a chance to flourish in a loving home. We encourage society to abandon preconceived notions and instead view rescue dogs as potential companions who can bring immense joy and loyalty to their lives.

Additionally, our book speaks directly to the government, urging them to act. We advocate for the implementation of stricter regulations and increased funding to improve shelter conditions. By investing in better facilities, increased staff training, and enrichment programs, we can alleviate the struggles faced by rescue dogs and provide them with a more conducive environment for rehabilitation and adoption.

This book enlightens pet owners, society, and the government about the challenges faced by rescue dogs in America. By understanding these struggles, we can collectively work towards improving the lives of these dogs and increasing their chances of finding forever homes. Let us unite in advocating for change and giving voice to those who cannot speak for themselves. Together, we can make a difference in the lives of rescue dogs and create a more compassionate society.

The Impact of Neglect and Abuse

Rescue dogs in America often come from heartbreaking backgrounds of neglect and abuse. This enlightenment for dogs aims to shed light on the profound impact these experiences have on these innocent animals. By understanding the effects of neglect and abuse, we can work together to provide the support and care these rescue dogs desperately need.

Neglect and abuse have severe consequences on the physical and emotional well-being of rescue dogs. Physically, neglected dogs often suffer from malnutrition, untreated medical conditions, and lack of proper exercise. The scars of abuse, both visible and invisible, can haunt these dogs long after they have been rescued. Emotionally, they may exhibit fear, anxiety, aggression, or withdrawal due to the trauma they have endured. The impact of neglect and abuse on dogs is a heartbreaking testament to the vulnerability and resilience of these loyal companions. Neglect, manifested through the deprivation of basic necessities such as food, shelter, and medical care, inflicts both physical and psychological wounds. Emaciated bodies and vacant eyes tell a tale of survival against the odds. The emotional toll is equally profound, with neglected dogs often exhibiting fear, anxiety, and a profound mistrust of humans.

On the other end of this spectrum lies the sinister realm of abuse, where the very beings meant to provide solace become sources of torment. Physical abuse leaves scars, both visible and hidden, altering a dog's physical well-being, and shattering its sense of security. Beyond the immediate physical trauma, the psychological scars of abuse can endure, leading to behavioral issues that make reintegration into a loving home a formidable challenge. Abused dogs may flinch at a raised hand, cower in fear, or struggle with basic social interactions. The impact is not only individual but echoes through communities, as these dogs may pose a risk to themselves and others.

However, amid the darkness, there exists a glimmer of hope. Dogs possess an astonishing capacity for forgiveness and healing. With patient care, positive reinforcement, and the warmth of a compassionate human touch, many abused and neglected dogs can embark on a transformative journey toward recovery. The transformative power of love and understanding can mend shattered spirits, proving that, even in the wake of cruelty, the indomitable spirit of dogs can prevail, and they can emerge as resilient, trusting companions ready to embrace the kindness they were so long denied. For pet owners, it is crucial to recognize the impact of neglect and abuse when adopting a rescue dog. Patience, understanding, and a nurturing environment are key to helping these dogs heal and regain trust. Proper training, socialization, and consistent care can help them overcome their past traumas and become loving family members.

Society must aid in raising awareness about the prevalence of neglect and abuse, we can encourage responsible pet ownership and discourage cruelty towards animals. Support for local animal shelters and rescue organizations is also crucial to ensure these dogs receive the care and rehabilitation they need. Strict legislation and enforcement are necessary to hold perpetrators accountable and prevent further harm to these vulnerable animals. Funding for animal welfare organizations and initiatives can also help provide better resources and education for both pet owners and the general public.

Neglect and abuse have a profound impact on rescue dogs in America. By understanding the physical and emotional consequences of these experiences, we can work together as pet owners, society, and the government to provide the necessary support and care for these dogs. Through awareness, responsible ownership, and legislative action, we can advocate for the voiceless and ensure that rescue dogs in America receive the love and compassion they deserve. Let us stand together and make a difference in the lives of these incredible animals.

Chapter 2: The Importance of Rescue Dog Adoption

Understanding the Benefits of Rescue Dogs

Rescue dogs have become an integral part of our society, providing immense benefits not only to their owners but also to the entire community. Let's explore the various advantages of adopting a rescue dog and shed light on the positive impact they have on saving rescue dogs in America. Understanding the benefits of rescue dogs unveils a tapestry of compassion, resilience, and untapped potential. These canine companions, often overlooked in shelters, bring a unique set of qualities that transcend their tumultuous pasts. One of the most profound benefits lies in the sheer act of giving a second chance. Rescue dogs, having faced adversity and abandonment, exhibit an unparalleled gratitude and loyalty when welcomed into a loving home. Their journey from neglect to the warmth of a caring family showcases their resilience and capacity for healing.

For pet owners, rescue dogs offer a unique and fulfilling bond. These dogs often come from difficult backgrounds, having faced abandonment, abuse, or neglect. By welcoming them into our homes, we not only provide them with a second chance at life but also experience the joy of witnessing their incredible transformation. Rescue dogs have an unparalleled ability to show gratitude and loyalty, creating an unbreakable bond with their owners. They teach us the value of resilience, compassion, and the power of love.

Adopting a rescue dog fosters a sense of purpose for the adopter, knowing that they have played a pivotal role in rewriting the narrative for a once-marginalized life. Beyond the emotional connection, rescue dogs often surprise with their intelligence, adaptability, and unwavering loyalty. Many of these dogs have faced challenges that demand resilience, making them particularly adept at overcoming obstacles and forming strong bonds with their human companions. The diversity among rescue dogs, encompassing various breeds, sizes, and personalities, ensures that there's a perfect match for individuals or families of all walks of life. The act of adopting a rescue dog contributes directly to the alleviation of shelter overcrowding, giving another dog the chance to find its forever home.

In a world that can sometimes feel chaotic, the presence of a rescue dog brings a profound sense of joy and purpose. Their ability to transform a house into a home, to be a steadfast companion through life's ups and downs, is a testament to the transformative power of love and compassion. Thus, the benefits of rescue dogs extend far beyond the individual bond—they radiate through families and communities, illustrating the beauty of second chances and the immense value these resilient creatures bring to our lives.

Rescuing dogs can provide a significant positive impact on our society as a whole. By adopting a rescue dog, we contribute to reducing the number of dogs in overcrowded shelters, thereby alleviating the strain on limited resources. This, in turn, allows shelters to focus on providing better care and rehabilitation for the remaining animals. Additionally, adopting a rescue dog helps to combat the unethical practices of puppy mills and backyard breeders, promoting responsible pet ownership and animal welfare.

In advocating for rescue dogs in America, it is essential to involve the government and society at large. Government agencies can play a crucial role in supporting and promoting the adoption of rescue dogs by implementing policies that incentivize adoption, such as tax breaks or reduced licensing fees. They can also allocate funds to improve shelter conditions and increase awareness about the benefits of rescue dogs. Society, on the other hand, can actively participate by volunteering at local shelters, fostering rescue dogs, or sharing success stories to inspire others.

Saving rescue dogs in America is not just a noble cause; it has numerous benefits that directly impact pet owners, society, and the government. Understanding these benefits empowers us to advocate for rescue dogs and encourage others to consider adoption. By opening our hearts and homes to these deserving animals, we not only enrich our lives but also contribute to creating a more compassionate and humane society for all creatures, big and small.

Myth-Busting: Common Misconceptions about Rescue Dogs

Rescue dogs hold a special place in our hearts. These brave and resilient animals have often endured unimaginable hardships before finding their forever homes. Common misconceptions surrounding rescue dogs often cast a shadow over these remarkable animals, perpetuating myths that can hinder their chances of finding loving homes. One prevailing misconception is that all rescue dogs harbor behavioral issues. While it's true that some may have faced adversity, many rescue dogs are affectionate, well-behaved, and quick to adapt to their new environments. Each dog has a unique personality shaped by its experiences, and with patience and understanding, they can overcome past traumas.

Another misconception revolves around the belief that only older dogs end up in shelters. Contrary to this notion, shelters are home to dogs of all ages, including puppies. Potential adopters can find a wide range of ages, sizes, and breeds, allowing them to choose a companion that aligns with their lifestyle. Additionally, there is a misconception that all rescue dogs are mutts. While mixed breeds are indeed common in shelters, purebred dogs can also be found waiting for a second chance. Adopters often discover that rescue organizations offer a diverse array of breeds and mixes, providing an opportunity to welcome a specific type of dog into their homes.

The assumption that all rescue dogs are damaged goods may dissuade potential adopters. In reality, these dogs possess an incredible capacity for love and loyalty. With proper care, training, and patience, rescue dogs can blossom into devoted family members, dispelling the notion that they are irreparably scared. Challenging these misconceptions is essential in promoting the adoption of rescue dogs, allowing these deserving animals to rewrite their stories in the warm embrace of a caring home.

However, there are several misconceptions surrounding rescue dogs that need to be debunked. As a voice for animals, we can bust these myths and shed light on the truth about these incredible animals. Let's address these myths and understand their complexity:

Myth #1: Rescue dogs are damaged goods and have behavior issues.

This misconception couldn't be further from the truth. While it is true that some rescue dogs may have experienced trauma or neglect, it does not define their character. Most rescue dogs are incredibly resilient, and with the right love, care, and training, they can become loyal and well-behaved companions. Many rescue dogs go on to excel in therapy work, agility competitions, and even become service animals.

Myth #2: Rescue dogs are all mixed breeds and not as desirable as purebred dogs.

The belief that rescue dogs are solely mixed breeds is inaccurate. Shelters and rescue organizations often have a wide variety of purebred dogs waiting for adoption. Regardless of breed, rescue dogs offer unique personalities and charm that cannot be matched. Additionally, mixed breed dogs tend to have fewer health issues compared to purebreds due to their genetic diversity.

Myth #3: All rescue dogs are old or sick.

This myth perpetuates the misconception that rescue dogs are unwanted or damaged. While it's true that some rescue dogs may be older or have medical conditions, many of them are young and healthy. Shelters and rescue organizations have dogs of all ages, sizes, and temperaments, ensuring there is a perfect match for every potential pet owner.

Myth #4: Rescue dogs are not suitable for families with children.

On the contrary, rescue dogs can be excellent companions for families with children. Many rescue dogs have undergone temperament evaluations, making it easier for shelters to match them with suitable families. With proper training and socialization, rescue dogs can form strong bonds with children, teaching them empathy, responsibility, and compassion.

It is crucial for society to understand the truth about rescue dogs. By debunking these common misconceptions, we can encourage more people to adopt these deserving animals and give them the loving homes they deserve. Let us celebrate the resilience and strength of rescue dogs and work together to save more lives and create a brighter future for all dogs in America.

The Personal Rewards of Adopting a Rescue Dog

As pet owners, we have the power to make a positive impact on the lives of animals in need. One way to do this is by adopting a rescue dog. The personal rewards that come with opening your heart and home to a rescue dog. These rewards extend not only to the pet owners but also to society and the government, as we work together to save rescue dogs in America.

Adopting a rescue dog is a profoundly rewarding experience that extends far beyond the joy of bringing a new furry friend into one's life. One of the most poignant personal rewards is the sense of fulfillment derived from providing a loving home to a dog in need. Rescue dogs often come from challenging backgrounds and witnessing their transformation from a wary and uncertain state to a thriving, happy companion is a source of unparalleled satisfaction. The deep and genuine bond that develops between an adopter and a rescue dog fosters a unique connection, grounded in gratitude and loyalty.

The act of saving a life, offering a second chance, and witnessing the positive impact on the dog's overall well-being is an emotionally enriching journey that leaves a lasting imprint on the adopter's heart. Moreover, the daily companionship of a rescue dog contributes significantly to an individual's mental and emotional well-being. The unconditional love and devotion these dogs offer create a sense of purpose and reduce feelings of loneliness. The interactive nature of caring for a rescue dog promotes physical activity, encouraging daily walks and playtime, which in turn enhances the adopter's overall health.

The shared experiences and adventures with a rescue dog can strengthen social connections, as dog owners often find themselves part of a community of fellow enthusiasts. The personal rewards of adopting a rescue dog extend to the satisfaction of contributing to a broader cause—the alleviation of shelter overcrowding and the promotion of responsible pet ownership. By providing a home for a rescue dog, individuals actively participate in creating a brighter future for these animals and inspire others to consider adoption. In essence, adopting a rescue dog becomes a transformative journey, offering not only the joy of companionship but also the immeasurable satisfaction of making a positive difference in the life of a deserving canine companion.

When you choose to rescue a dog, you are giving a second chance to a deserving animal. The bond that forms between a rescued dog and its owner is often indescribable. These dogs have often experienced neglect, abuse, or abandonment, and when they find a loving home, they are forever grateful. The joy and unconditional love that a rescue dog brings into a home are immeasurable. Not only does adopting a rescue dog provide companionship, but it also teaches us compassion, patience, and the importance of giving back.

In addition to personal rewards, society benefits greatly from the adoption of rescue dogs. Each year, millions of dogs end up in overcrowded shelters, many of which are euthanized due to lack of space or resources. By adopting a rescue dog, you are directly contributing to reducing the number of animals in shelters and giving them a chance at a better life. This, in turn, helps alleviate the strain on animal welfare organizations and shelters, allowing them to focus their resources on other important tasks. Having more rescue dogs in loving homes helps create a compassionate society that values the well-being of all living creatures.

Government must support the cause of saving rescue dogs in America by advocating for policies that promote adoption and responsible pet ownership. Government law makers can help create a more favorable environment for rescue dogs. This includes implementing stricter regulations on breeding facilities, providing funding for spay/neuter programs, and supporting animal welfare organizations. The personal rewards of adopting a rescue dog extend to the government as well, as they witness the positive impact these animals have on individuals and communities.

Adopting a rescue dog is a rewarding experience on multiple levels. It brings immense joy and love into the lives of pet owners, contributes to a compassionate society, and demonstrates the government's commitment to animal welfare. By choosing to adopt, we can all be voices for the voiceless and make a difference in the lives of rescue dogs in America.

Chapter 3: The Role of Society in Rescuing Dogs

Fostering a Culture of Responsible Pet Ownership

In a society that values the well-being and happiness of all creatures, it is imperative to foster a culture of responsible pet ownership. It is important to shed light on the responsibility of pet ownership and its role in saving rescue dogs in America. Pet owners, society, and the government all play significant roles in ensuring the welfare of animals, particularly rescue dogs. By understanding the responsibilities associated with owning a pet, we can collectively create a safe and loving environment for these vulnerable creatures.

Fostering a culture of responsible pet ownership is a vital endeavor that transcends the individual and extends to the well-being of animals, communities, and society at large. At its core, responsible pet ownership involves a commitment to the comprehensive care and welfare of a companion animal throughout its lifetime. This begins with educated and informed decisions about pet selection, considering factors such as breed characteristics, size, and energy levels that align with an individual or family's lifestyle. Responsible pet owners prioritize spaying and neutering to curb overpopulation and reduce the number of animals ending up in shelters.

Responsible pet ownership encompasses the provision of proper nutrition, veterinary care, and regular exercise, ensuring a pet's physical health and mental well-being. Providing a safe and enriching environment that includes shelter, adequate living space, and mental stimulation is equally crucial. Pet owners committed to responsibility also understand the significance of training and socialization, fostering positive behaviors that contribute to harmonious interactions between pets and their communities. In promoting responsible pet ownership, education plays a pivotal role. This involves disseminating information about the financial and time commitments of pet ownership, the importance of identification through tags or micro-chipping, and the necessity of compliance with local animal welfare laws.

Responsible pet ownership also extends to the ethical treatment of animals, encouraging kindness, empathy, and the prevention of cruelty. Creating a culture that recognizes pets as lifelong companions rather than disposable possessions is essential for cultivating responsible attitudes. Ultimately, a society that embraces responsible pet ownership not only ensures the welfare of individual animals but also contributes to the overall well-being of communities. By championing education, compassion, and a commitment to the needs of our animal companions, we lay the foundation for a culture where pets thrive, enriching the lives of those who care for them and fostering a sense of responsibility that reverberates through generations.

As pet owners, we have the privilege and responsibility of providing our furry companions with the care they deserve. Responsible pet ownership begins with adopting rather than buying from pet stores or breeders. By adopting a rescue dog, we not only save a life but also make room for another dog in need. It is crucial to remember that owning a pet is a long-term commitment, and it requires time, dedication, and financial resources. Regular veterinary care, proper nutrition, exercise, and socialization are essential to ensure the well-being of our four-legged friends.

Through education and awareness campaigns, we can promote the importance of spaying and neutering pets to prevent overpopulation and reduce the number of dogs ending up in shelters. Additionally, society can encourage responsible ownership by promoting the benefits of training and socializing dogs. Well-trained dogs are more likely to be well-behaved, reducing the risk of abandonment or relinquishment.

The government is stepping up their responsibility by enacting and enforcing laws that protect animals from abuse, neglect, and cruelty. The government can ensure that owners are held accountable for their actions. Legislation can also promote the adoption of rescue dogs by offering incentives such as tax breaks or reduced licensing fees for rescued pets. Unfortunately, the government process can be slow and complex while dogs suffer at the expense of bureaucracy.

Fostering a culture of responsible pet ownership is a collective effort. By educating pet owners, advocating for animal welfare, and implementing effective legislation, we can create a society that not only saves rescue dogs but also celebrates the bond between humans and animals. Let our mission ensure that every pet is given the love, care, and respect they deserve be a priority.

Educating the Public on the Benefits of Rescue Dog Adoption

Rescue dog adoption is not just about providing a home for a furry companion; it is a decision that can have a profound impact on both the adopter and the rescue dog. Educating the public on the benefits of rescue dog adoption is a pivotal step toward transforming the lives of both humans and their potential four-legged companions. At the forefront of this awareness campaign is the recognition that rescue dogs bring a wealth of unique qualities and untapped potential to their adoptive homes. By dispelling the misconception that all rescue dogs are laden with behavioral issues, educational efforts emphasize the resilience, loyalty, and gratitude these dogs exhibit when given a second chance. The act of adopting a rescue dog not only saves a life but also fosters a deep, enduring bond between the adopter and the dog.

Public education underscores the diversity available in rescue organizations, debunking the myth that only older or mixed-breed dogs are found in shelters. Prospective adopters are introduced to a wide array of breeds, ages, and sizes, allowing them to find a perfect match that aligns with their lifestyle. By understanding that rescue dogs encompass a variety of backgrounds and temperaments, potential adopters are empowered to make informed decisions that resonate with their preferences and capabilities.

The public is educated on the broader impact of rescue dog adoption, emphasizing the positive ripple effect on shelter populations and the community at large. Choosing to adopt a rescue dog directly contributes to the alleviation of overcrowded shelters, creating space for more dogs to find homes. The public is encouraged to view rescue dog adoption not only as a personal decision but as a collective effort to address the broader issues of pet overpopulation and animal welfare. Through these educational initiatives, the public is inspired to see rescue dog adoption not just as an altruistic act but as a transformative journey that enriches lives, fosters companionship, and contributes to the creation of a more compassionate and humane society.

Rescue dog adoption offers a unique opportunity to save a life while gaining a loving and loyal companion. Many rescue dogs have faced challenging circumstances such as abuse, neglect, or abandonment, and by providing them with a forever home, pet owners become part of their journey towards healing and happiness. Rescue dogs often exhibit a deep sense of gratitude, forming an unbreakable bond with their adopters. Adopting a rescue dog can also be a transformative experience for pet owners, as it enhances their sense of empathy, compassion, and responsibility.

Everyone can benefit from rescue dog adoption in numerous ways. Firstly, by adopting a rescue dog, individuals alleviate the strain on overcrowded shelters and rescue organizations, allowing them to focus on saving more lives. Additionally, rescue dog adoption promotes a culture of compassion and responsible pet ownership within communities. By choosing adoption over purchasing from breeders or pet stores, society sends a powerful message that all animals deserve a second chance. Educating the public about the benefits of rescue dog adoption can also help dispel common myths surrounding shelter animals, such as behavioral issues or health problems, and encourage more people to consider adopting rather than buying.

Government involvement in promoting and supporting adoption programs, government entities can help reduce the number of stray and abandoned dogs, ultimately leading to a decrease in euthanasia rates. Legislation that supports the adoption of rescue dogs, such as tax incentives or mandatory spaying and neutering programs, can also contribute to a more compassionate society. Furthermore, public funding for shelters and rescue organizations can ensure that they have the necessary resources to provide proper care and rehabilitation for rescue dogs.

Educating the public on the benefits of rescue dog adoption is essential for creating a society that values and advocates for the well-being of rescue dogs. By raising awareness among pet owners, society, and government entities, we can save more lives, promote responsible pet ownership, and create a more compassionate world for our four-legged friends.

Creating Supportive Communities for Rescue Dog Owners

Rescuing dogs is an essential part of our society, providing companionship, love, and loyalty to their owners. However, being a rescue dog owner comes with its own unique set of challenges. These challenges can be overcome by creating supportive communities that understand and address the needs of rescue dog owners. As we create supportive communities, let us do it through karmatic measures that will inspire others to participate.

First and foremost, creating supportive communities for rescue dog owners is crucial because it helps in sharing knowledge and experiences. Rescue dogs often come from difficult backgrounds, and their owners may face specific issues related to their history, behavior, and health. By fostering a sense of community, owners can exchange valuable information, tips, and advice on how to provide the best care for their rescue dogs. This collective knowledge can greatly benefit both new and experienced owners, leading to better overall welfare for rescue dogs.

Supportive communities provide emotional support to rescue dog owners. Owning a rescue dog can be emotionally challenging, especially when dealing with the trauma and behavioral issues that some of these dogs may have. By connecting with others who are going through similar experiences, owners can find solace, understanding, and encouragement. This emotional support system acts as a lifeline, preventing feelings of isolation and ensuring that rescue dog owners can cope with the challenges they face.

Supportive communities also play a crucial role in raising awareness and educating society about rescue dogs. By organizing events, workshops, and awareness campaigns, these communities can help dispel myths and prejudices associated with rescue dogs. They can promote responsible pet ownership, encourage adoption, and emphasize the benefits of providing a loving home to a rescue dog.

Furthermore, governments can benefit from these communities by collaborating with them to develop and implement policies that protect the rights and welfare of rescue dogs. By working together, governments and supportive communities can create legislation that promotes responsible breeding practices, ensures the availability of resources for rescues, and establishes better standards for animal shelters.

Creating supportive communities for rescue dog owners is essential for the well-being of both the owners and their pets. These communities foster knowledge sharing, emotional support, awareness, and collaboration with the government. Society can make a significant difference in the lives of rescue dogs, ultimately striving towards the shared goal of saving rescue dogs in America.

Chapter 4: Government Initiatives for Rescue Dog Welfare

Current Policies and Regulations on Rescue Dog Adoption

Over the past 20 years, the issue of rescue dog adoption has gained significant attention in America. As more and more people become aware of the plight of abandoned and neglected dogs, there has been an increasing demand for policies and regulations to protect and promote the welfare of these animals. Let's examine the current policies and regulations on rescue dog adoption in America, addressing the interests of pet owners, society, and the government.

Federal organizations like the U.S. Department of Agriculture (USDA) oversee commercial breeders and certain animal facilities to ensure compliance with the Animal Welfare Act. At the state and local levels, animal shelters and rescue organizations are often subject to regulations governing licensing, inspections, and care standards. These regulations aim to safeguard the health and welfare of animals in their care. Common requirements include providing adequate veterinary care, proper nutrition, and suitable living conditions for animals awaiting adoption. Adoption policies for rescue dogs typically involve a thorough screening process to ensure the well-being of both the animals and the adoptive families. This process may include background checks, interviews, and home visits. Adoption fees are often applied to cover veterinary care, spaying/neutering, and other expenses related to the dog's care.

Micro-chipping and identification are frequently mandated to increase the chances of reuniting lost dogs with their owners and to discourage irresponsible breeding or abandonment. Some regions may also have restrictions on the types of animals that can be adopted, emphasizing responsible ownership.

One of the primary concerns in rescue dog adoption is ensuring the safety and well-being of both the dogs and the adopters. Many states have implemented mandatory spaying and neutering programs to control the population of stray dogs and prevent further over breeding. These programs not only reduce the number of unwanted dogs but also help prevent certain health issues associated with intact animals. Additionally, most rescue organizations require potential adopters to undergo a screening process, including interviews and home visits, to ensure that the dogs are placed in suitable environments.

To further protect the welfare of rescue dogs, various states have enacted anti-cruelty laws. These laws make it a criminal offense to mistreat, neglect, or abandon animals, including rescue dogs. The penalties for such offenses range from fines to imprisonment, depending on the severity of the abuse. These regulations send a strong message that animal cruelty will not be tolerated and provide legal recourse for rescue dogs subjected to mistreatment.

There has also been a push for increased transparency and accountability within the rescue dog adoption process. Many organizations now require detailed documentation of a dog's medical history, behavior assessment, and any known issues. This information not only helps potential adopters make informed decisions but also ensures that rescue dogs are placed in homes where they can receive the appropriate care and support.

The government has recognized the importance of rescue dog adoption and has introduced several initiatives to support these efforts. This includes funding for animal shelters, spay/neuter programs, and public education campaigns. By investing in these initiatives, the government aims to reduce the number of homeless dogs and promote responsible pet ownership. It's important to note that the landscape of policies and regulations on rescue dog adoptions may evolve, with changes occurring at the federal, state, and local levels.

Staying informed about local regulations and collaborating with reputable rescue organizations helps ensure that both animals and adopters are protected through responsible and ethical adoption practices. For the latest and most accurate information, individuals interested in rescue dog adoption should contact local animal shelters, rescue groups, and relevant government agencies.

The current policies and regulations on rescue dog adoption in America reflect a growing commitment to the welfare and well-being of these animals. Through mandatory spaying and neutering programs, anti-cruelty laws, increased transparency, and government support, efforts are being made to address the issues surrounding rescue dog adoption. However, there is always room for improvement, and continued advocacy and awareness are crucial to ensure that rescue dogs in America find loving and permanent homes.

The Need for Stricter Animal Welfare Laws

The issue of animal welfare has gained significant attention and has become a topic of concern for many animal lovers. Pet owners play a crucial role in ensuring the well-being of their furry friends. However, the sad reality is that not all pet owners treat their animals with the care and respect they deserve. Many rescue dogs have suffered from neglect, abuse, and abandonment. Stricter animal welfare laws can help address these issues by providing a legal framework that holds irresponsible pet owners accountable for their actions.

Society as a whole has a moral obligation to advocate for the protection of rescue dogs. By implementing stricter animal welfare laws, we can send a clear message that animal cruelty will not be tolerated. These laws can serve as a deterrent, preventing potential abusers from engaging in harmful behaviors towards animals. Furthermore, they can help educate the public about responsible pet ownership and the importance of treating all animals with compassion and empathy.

The government could enhance its commitment to protecting vulnerable creatures. Increasing forcible measures on laws that establish guidelines for the treatment and care of animals can ensure that they have access to essential resources such as food, water, shelter, and veterinary care. They can also increase penalties for those who violate these laws, discouraging acts of cruelty and neglect.

By focusing on saving rescue dogs in America, we address a specific niche that requires immediate attention. Rescue dogs often come from traumatic backgrounds, having experienced abuse, homelessness, or neglect. Stricter animal welfare laws can provide essential safeguards for these vulnerable animals, ensuring that they are given the opportunity to heal, rehabilitate, and find loving forever homes.

The need for stricter animal welfare laws cannot be overstated. By implementing these laws, pet owners, society, and the government can work together to create a safer and more compassionate environment for all animals, including rescue dogs. It is our collective responsibility to be the voice for the voiceless and advocate for the rights and welfare of these innocent creatures.

Promoting Rescue Dog Adoption through Legislation

The issue of abandoned and neglected dogs in America has reached alarming proportions. Thousands of innocent lives are lost every day due to the lack of responsible pet ownership and the absence of adequate legislation to protect these voiceless creatures. It is crucial for pet owners, society, and the government to come together and address this pressing concern. The significance of implementing specific laws and regulations to safeguard the lives of rescue dogs and encourage their adoption would have a substantial impact on the overall well-being of rescue dogs.

Rescue dog adoption can bring about transformative changes in both the lives of these animals and the families who provide them with a loving home. However, to create a more favorable environment for rescue dogs, we must focus on creating and enforcing legislation that promotes their adoption. One of the first steps is to establish mandatory spaying and neutering laws nationwide. This would effectively reduce the number of unwanted litter and significantly decrease the burden on animal shelters and rescue organizations.

Through implementing stricter regulations on puppy mills and backyard breeders could be paramount in the success of slowing populations. These unregulated breeding operations often prioritize profit over the welfare of animals, leading to overpopulation, genetic health issues, and poor living conditions. By enforcing laws that impose strict standards for breeding facilities and ensuring regular inspections, we can mitigate the suffering endured by countless dogs and encourage prospective pet owners to adopt from shelters instead.

Also, promoting rescue dog adoption through tax incentives and financial benefits can encourage more families to consider adopting rather than purchasing from pet stores or breeders. Governments can offer tax deductions for expenses related to the care and adoption of rescue dogs, such as veterinary bills, training costs, and adoption fees. By providing these incentives, society and the government acknowledge the value of rescue dogs and encourage their adoption as a responsible and compassionate choice.

Education and awareness programs should also be an integral part of promoting rescue dog adoption. By incorporating animal welfare education into school curricula and organizing community events that emphasize the benefits of adopting rescue dogs, we can foster a culture of empathy and responsibility towards these animals. Furthermore, disseminating information about the adoption process, the benefits of rescue dogs, and success stories can help dispel myths and misconceptions surrounding shelter animals.

Promoting rescue dog adoption through legislation is crucial to addressing the growing crisis of abandoned and neglected dogs in America. By implementing mandatory spaying and neutering laws, regulating breeding operations, offering financial incentives, and promoting education and awareness, we can create a society that values the lives of rescue dogs and actively supports their adoption. It is our collective responsibility as a society to save and improve the lives of these deserving animals.

Chapter 5: The Challenges of Rescue Dog Rehabilitation

Addressing Behavioral Issues in Rescue Dogs

Rescue dogs plays a vital role in our society by offering companionship, love, and loyalty to their owners. However, many of these incredible animals come with a unique set of challenges due to their previous experiences. Addressing behavioral issues in rescue dogs is a compassionate and essential aspect of ensuring their successful integration into loving homes. Many rescue dogs come from varied backgrounds, and their past experiences may contribute to behavioral challenges such as fear, anxiety, or mistrust.

One of the first steps in addressing behavioral issues in rescue dogs is to understand the underlying causes. Many rescue dogs have experienced trauma, neglect, or abuse, which can profoundly impact their behavior. By recognizing their past and empathizing with their struggles, we can approach training and rehabilitation with patience and compassion. We must recognize that each dog is an individual with unique needs and sensitivities. Professional guidance from trainers or behaviorists can be invaluable in creating tailored rehabilitation plans that focus on positive reinforcement and building trust.

Proper training is crucial for rescue dogs, as it helps them build trust, develop new skills, and overcome behavioral challenges. Pet owners should seek professional guidance from experienced dog trainers who specialize in working with rescue dogs. These experts can create tailored training plans that address specific issues such as fear, anxiety, aggression, or separation anxiety. Through consistent positive reinforcement, these dogs can learn new behaviors and regain confidence.

Positive reinforcement techniques, such as rewarding desirable behaviors with treats or praise, can effectively encourage positive habits and discourage unwanted behaviors. Consistency and patience in training sessions are key to reinforcing positive changes over time. Understanding that behavioral issues may be rooted in past traumas, adopters are encouraged to approach their new companions with empathy and compassion. Recognizing small victories, celebrating progress, and building a strong bond through positive interactions contribute to a sense of security for the rescue dog.

In some cases, seeking the guidance of veterinary professionals to rule out underlying health issues influencing behavior is essential. By taking a holistic approach that combines patience, positive reinforcement, professional guidance, and a deep understanding of the individual dog's history, adopters can play a transformative role in helping rescue dogs overcome behavioral challenges and thrive in their new homes.

Consistent and structured routines play a pivotal role in helping rescue dogs feel secure and acclimate to their new environments. Establishing clear boundaries, providing a safe space, and offering a predictable routine help address anxiety and uncertainty. Socialization, exposure to different environments, and gradual introductions to new people and animals are crucial elements in helping rescue dogs overcome fear and build confidence.

Socialization is another essential aspect of addressing behavioral issues in rescue dogs. Many of these animals may have had limited exposure to different environments, people, and other animals. Gradual and controlled introductions to new experiences can help them feel more comfortable and reduce anxiety. Encouraging positive interactions with other dogs and people can improve their social skills and overall well-being.

It is crucial for society to recognize the importance of rescue dogs and the challenges they face. By raising awareness, we can promote responsible pet ownership and encourage people to adopt rather than purchase dogs. Society can support rescue organizations by volunteering, donating, or fostering dogs in need. Additionally, government support through funding and legislation can help improve the welfare of rescue dogs and ensure they receive the care and rehabilitation they require.

Addressing behavioral issues in rescue dogs requires a multifaceted approach involving pet owners, society, and the government. By understanding the root causes of these issues, providing proper training and socialization, and advocating for the welfare of rescue dogs, we can help these incredible animals overcome their past experiences and thrive in their new homes.

Providing Medical Care and Rehabilitation

In our journey of advocating for rescue dogs in America, one of the most critical aspects is ensuring their well-being through proper medical care and rehabilitation. Rescue dogs often come from challenging backgrounds, having endured neglect, abuse, or abandonment. As pet owners, society, and the government, it is our collective responsibility to step up and provide these incredible beings with the care and support they need to lead healthy and happy lives.

Medical care forms the foundation of any rehabilitation process. When a rescue dog is brought into a shelter or a loving home, a thorough veterinary examination is crucial. This examination allows us to identify any underlying health issues, including physical injuries, infections, or chronic conditions, that may require immediate attention. Regular check-ups and vaccinations are equally important to ensure their long-term well-being.

Unfortunately, many rescue dogs suffer from psychological trauma due to their past experiences. These dogs may exhibit fearful or aggressive behavior, making it imperative to provide rehabilitation aimed at healing their emotional wounds. Collaborating with professional trainers and behaviorists can help identify specific needs, design tailored training programs, and work towards re-socializing these dogs, enabling them to trust humans again.

Rehabilitation centers and animal shelters play a vital role in providing medical care and rehabilitation to rescue dogs. These facilities serve as safe havens for these vulnerable animals, offering them specialized services and individual attention. By supporting and volunteering at these centers, we can contribute to the physical and emotional recovery of these dogs. Raising awareness about the importance of adopting rescue dogs and providing them with the necessary medical care can help reduce the burden on these facilities and encourage more people to open their hearts and homes to these deserving animals.

The government can support this endeavor by allocating resources and implementing legislation that ensures the welfare of rescue dogs. The government can play a significant role in improving their lives. This could include funding veterinary care, supporting rehabilitation programs, and enforcing stricter regulations against animal cruelty.

Together we have the power to make a difference in the lives of rescue dogs. By providing them with comprehensive medical care and rehabilitation, we can ensure that they have a second chance at a happy and fulfilling life. Let us stand united in our commitment to saving rescue dogs in America and advocating for their well-being.

Overcoming Trauma: Emotional Healing for Rescue Dogs

Rescue dogs in America often come from challenging and traumatic backgrounds. They may have experienced abuse, neglect, or abandonment, leaving them with deep emotional scars. It is our responsibility to address these issues and help these dogs heal. Emotional healing plays a vital role in the rehabilitation of rescue dogs. Just like humans, dogs can suffer from post-traumatic stress disorder (PTSD) and other emotional disorders. These conditions can manifest in various ways, such as fear, anxiety, aggression, or withdrawal. By understanding and addressing their emotional needs, we can create an environment that fosters healing and recovery.

One crucial aspect of emotional healing is providing a safe and stable environment. This includes a comfortable living space, regular routines, and consistent positive reinforcement. Creating a predictable and secure environment helps these dogs regain trust in humans and reduces their anxiety levels.

Socialization with other dogs and humans is key to their emotional rehabilitation. Encouraging positive interactions and gradually exposing them to different environments helps them overcome fears and build confidence. Professional trainers and behaviorists can play a crucial role in this process, providing guidance and support to both the dog and their owners.

Another essential tool for emotional healing is the implementation of therapeutic activities. These may include exercises like obedience training, puzzle games, and interactive playtime. Such activities not only stimulate their minds but also promote bonding and trust-building between the dog and their owner.

By incorporating relaxation techniques like massage, aromatherapy, and music therapy can help soothe their anxiety and promote a sense of well-being. These techniques have been proven to reduce stress levels in both humans and animals, facilitating the healing process.

It is crucial for society and the government to support initiatives that advocate for the emotional healing of rescue dogs. This can involve funding research on trauma recovery in animals, promoting legislation that ensures proper treatment for rescue animals, and raising awareness about the importance of adopting and fostering rescue dogs.

Emotional healing is a fundamental aspect of rehabilitating rescue dogs in America. By providing a safe environment, socialization, therapeutic activities, and support from society and the government, we can help these dogs overcome their traumatic pasts and lead happy, fulfilling lives. Let us be a voice for the voiceless and advocate for the emotional well-being of rescue dogs across America.

Chapter 6: Advocacy and Activism for Rescue Dogs

Spreading Awareness through Social Media Campaigns

In this digital age, social media has emerged as a powerful tool for spreading awareness and advocating for causes that are close to our hearts. When it comes to saving rescue dogs in America, social media campaigns have proven to be a game-changer in generating support, raising funds, and ultimately making a difference in the lives of these voiceless creatures. By harnessing the power of social media, we can effectively reach out to these audiences, educate them about the challenges faced by rescue dogs, and inspire them to act.

One of the key advantages of social media campaigns is their ability to engage and connect with a vast and diverse audience. Through compelling visuals, heartwarming stories, and informative content, we can create a virtual community of pet owners and animal lovers who are passionate about saving rescue dogs. By sharing success stories, highlighting the struggles faced by rescue dogs, and showcasing the incredible transformations they undergo, we can evoke empathy and encourage people to become advocates for these animals.

Social media campaigns also provide an excellent platform for fundraising and generating support. By partnering with local shelters, rescue organizations, and government agencies, we can organize online fundraising events, virtual adoption drives, and awareness campaigns that encourage people to donate, volunteer, and adopt rescue dogs. Such campaigns can create a ripple effect, inspiring others to get involved and make a meaningful impact on the lives of these animals.

Social media can be a powerful tool for influencing government policies and regulations surrounding rescue dogs. By leveraging the collective voice of pet owners and society at large, we can petition for stricter animal welfare laws, increased funding for animal shelters, and better resources for rescue organizations. Social media campaigns can serve as a platform for raising awareness about these issues, mobilizing public support, and pressuring lawmakers to prioritize the well-being of rescue dogs.

Passionate social media campaigns have revolutionized the way we advocate for and save rescue dogs in America. By utilizing the power of social media, we can spread awareness, generate support, and inspire action among pet owners, society, and the government. Humans are the guiding light for creating a brighter future for rescue dogs in America.

Collaborating with Rescue Organizations and Shelters

Rescue dogs are often the forgotten souls of our society, but they deserve a chance at a happy and fulfilling life just like any other pet. In order to make a difference in the lives of these voiceless creatures, it would be a selfless act on our part to collaborate with rescue organizations and shelters.

Rescue organizations and shelters play a vital role in saving and rehabilitating abandoned, abused, and neglected dogs. These dedicated organizations work tirelessly to provide medical care, foster homes, and training for these animals, giving them a second chance at life. By collaborating with these organizations, pet owners can make a significant impact on the number of rescue dogs in America.

One way pet owners can collaborate is by considering adoption instead of purchasing a dog from a breeder. Rescue organizations and shelters have a wide variety of dogs available for adoption, ranging from puppies to older dogs, and from various breeds to mixed breeds. By adopting a rescue dog, pet owners not only save a life but also open up space in shelters for other dogs in need.

Society can proactively raise awareness about the importance of rescue dogs and help change the negative perception that rescue dogs are damaged or inferior. Through education campaigns, community events, and media outreach, society can promote the benefits of adopting rescue dogs and highlight the success stories of these amazing animals.

Government involvement is also essential to address the challenges faced by rescue organizations and shelters. By providing funding, implementing stricter laws against animal cruelty, and supporting spay/neuter programs, the government can significantly impact the number of rescue dogs in America. Collaboration between the government and rescue organizations can also lead to the creation of more effective adoption procedures, ensuring that rescue dogs find loving and permanent homes.

Collaborating with rescue organizations and shelters is essential for saving rescue dogs in America. Pet owners can make a difference by adopting rather than purchasing a dog, while society can raise awareness about the benefits of rescue dogs. Government involvement is vital in providing funding and implementing laws to protect these animals. I would like to challenge society and government officials to take time out of their busy schedules to volunteer at a local shelter or rescue today.

Fundraising for Rescue Dog Initiatives

The issue of rescue dogs in America has gained significant attention over the past 2 decades. These innocent animals find themselves abandoned, neglected, or mistreated, desperately longing for a second chance at life. Fortunately, there are countless organizations and individuals dedicated to saving and rehabilitating these helpless creatures. However, the work of these rescue initiatives cannot be sustained without the crucial support of the community. Let's shed some light on the importance of fundraising for rescue dog initiatives and encourage pet owners, society, and the government to get involved.

Rescue dog initiatives face numerous challenges, including limited resources, lack of funding, and overwhelming demands. Fundraising plays a pivotal role in addressing these obstacles and providing the necessary support for these organizations to continue their life-saving mission. By organizing fundraisers, every individual has the power to contribute to the larger cause of saving rescue dogs in America.

Pet owners are at the forefront of this movement. Many of them have experienced firsthand the joy and unconditional love that rescue dogs bring into their lives. By mobilizing fellow pet owners within their communities, these proactive dog lovers can organize events such as dog walks, pet shows, or pet-themed auctions to raise funds for local rescue organizations. Dog lovers can donate a portion of the proceeds from pet-related businesses, such as grooming salons or pet supply stores, to support these initiatives.

Society has a responsibility to protect the voiceless and vulnerable. Individuals who may not own pets can still play a significant role in fundraising for rescue dog initiatives. Donating to reputable rescue organizations, volunteering at local shelters, or supporting online crowdfunding campaigns are just a few ways society can contribute. By spreading awareness through social media platforms or hosting educational events, individuals can help dispel misconceptions surrounding rescue dogs and encourage adoption.

Our government must play a crucial role in supporting rescue dog initiatives. Allocating funds to local shelters, enacting legislation to promote responsible pet ownership, or offering tax incentives to individuals who adopt rescue dogs are some ways the government can contribute. By recognizing the importance of rescue dog initiatives and actively supporting them, the government can make a significant impact on the lives of countless dogs in need.

Fundraising for rescue dog initiatives is essential to saving rescue dogs in America. Pet owners, society, and the government all have a role to play in supporting these initiatives. We can provide rescue dogs the second chance they deserve, offering them love, care, and a forever home. Always remember the basic laws of love, you are only able to receive what you are willing to give.

Chapter 7: Success Stories: Inspiring Tales of Rescue Dog Rehabilitation

From Neglect to Love: Transformations of Rescued Dogs

Rescue dogs have a unique story to tell, one that often begins with neglect and ends with unconditional love. Let us be inspired by the incredible journey these dogs undertake, and the profound impact they can have on our lives. This chapter is dedicated to pet owners, society, and the government, urging them to recognize the importance of saving rescue dogs in America.

Rescued dogs come from a variety of backgrounds, ranging from puppy mills to abusive households or simply being abandoned on the streets. They arrive at shelters broken, scared, and often in need of medical attention. However, with the right care and love, these dogs have the potential to undergo remarkable transformations.

For pet owners, adopting a rescue dog can be a life-changing experience. These dogs are incredibly grateful for a second chance and, once given the opportunity, they blossom into loyal and affectionate companions. Their resilience and capacity to forgive is truly remarkable. By sharing heartwarming stories of rescue dog adoptions, we hope to inspire more pet owners to consider adopting from shelters rather than purchasing from breeders.

It is essential to raise awareness about the plight of these animals and dispel the misconceptions surrounding them. By highlighting the incredible transformations of rescue dogs, we aim to challenge the stigma associated with them and promote a more compassionate attitude towards these deserving creatures. Furthermore, we emphasize the importance of supporting local shelters and rescues financially and through volunteer work.

Dog lovers continuously advocate for stronger animal welfare laws, stricter regulations for breeding facilities, and increased funding for animal shelters. By prioritizing the needs of rescue dogs, the government can make a significant impact in reducing animal suffering and promoting responsible pet ownership. Communication with our local, state, and federal advocates can make a major impact on gaining support for our furry loved ones.

This book will hopefully shed light on the incredible journeys these animals embark upon. Through adopting rescue dogs, pet owners can experience the joy of transforming the lives of these deserving creatures. By educating society and advocating for changes in government policies, we can collectively work towards a future where every rescue dog finds a loving home.

The Healing Power of Adoption: Stories of Rescued Dogs and their Owners

Across America, rescue dogs are often overlooked or forgotten, left to suffer in shelters or on the streets. This heartwarming message provides readers a look into the transformative journeys of pet owners and their rescued dogs. This section showcases the profound impact that adoption has on both the lives of these dogs and their human counterparts. Through heartfelt tales of resilience, love, and redemption, we explore how these once abandoned or neglected animals have become beacons of hope, healing, and joy.

Through the lens of various perspectives, we witness the remarkable transformation that occurs when a rescue dog finds its forever home. From the bond that forms between a traumatized dog and its patient owner, to the newfound purpose and companionship that rescue dogs bring to their families, these stories exemplify the profound impact that adoption has on both the dog and its human counterpart.

Moreover, we examine the broader societal implications of rescue dog adoption. By advocating for the importance of saving rescue dogs in America, we highlight the potential benefits for society at large. Studies have shown that pet ownership can lead to improved mental and physical well-being, decreased stress levels, and increased social integration. By encouraging adoption, we not only improve the lives of individual animals but also contribute to the overall well-being of our communities.

We call upon pet owners, society, and government to recognize and support the vital work of rescue organizations and individuals who tirelessly advocate for these animals. By sharing these inspiring stories, we hope to foster a deeper understanding of the healing power of adoption and the tremendous positive impact it has on the lives of both rescue dogs and their owners.

Join us as we celebrate the extraordinary journeys of these once-forgotten dogs and their compassionate owners. Through their stories, we aim to inspire change, compassion, and a collective commitment to saving rescue dogs in America. Together, we can make a difference and give voice to the voiceless.

Enjoy these stories of companionship and love with all your heart:

1. *From Neglect to Companionship:* Sarah rescued a neglected and malnourished dog named Max from a local shelter. As Max regained his health, he became Sarah's steadfast companion, providing emotional support during her difficult times and bringing joy into her life. They both now find hope and meaning in life again.

2. *A Healing Bond:* Mark, a military veteran, adopted a rescue dog named Bella. Bella's affectionate nature and companionship played a pivotal role in Mark's emotional healing from PTSD, providing comfort and understanding during his challenging post-service transition back into society.

3. *Unconditional Love in Retirement:* After retiring, Linda adopted Buddy, a senior rescue dog. Buddy's gentle demeanor and unwavering loyalty filled Linda's days with purpose and joy, making her retirement years fulfilling and meaningful. They traveled the world making memories creating a long-lasting bond.

4. *Therapeutic Tail Wagger:* Emily, a therapist, adopted a rescue dog named Bailey as a therapy animal for her clients. Bailey's presence has had a remarkable impact, offering comfort and support to those in need and enhancing the therapeutic environment. She not only found happiness with Bailey, but she also found purpose in Bailey to help others.

5. *From Shy to Social Butterfly:* When Alex adopted Luna, a shy rescue dog, they embarked on a journey of socialization and confidence-building. Luna's transformation from a timid pup to a social and outgoing companion enriched both of their lives. Alex takes Luna everywhere he goes and everyone they encounter adores Luna's personality.

6. *Adventure Buddies for Life:* Jack, an avid hiker, adopted Rocky, a high-energy rescue dog. Together, they explored countless trails and mountains, creating an unbreakable bond and transforming Jack's passion for adventure into a shared, lifelong journey. Their journey together has been a beacon of light for others to follow.

7. *Furry Co-Worker and Stress Reliever:* Working from home became more enjoyable for Rachel when she adopted Max, a rescue dog. Max's presence alleviated stress, provided companionship during long hours, and turned the home office into a welcoming and positive space. She finds her time more productive and enjoyable with a loyal companion at her side.

8. *Rescue Dog, Rescuer's Best Friend:* After adopting Cooper, a playful rescue dog, Amy found herself becoming more active and engaged in outdoor activities. Cooper's enthusiasm for life inspired Amy to live more fully, fostering a healthier and more vibrant lifestyle. They visit the local park daily to enjoy nature and take time to reflect on their bond.

9. *The Joy of Second Chances:* Tom and his family adopted Jake, a senior rescue dog with health issues. Despite Jake's challenges, the joy he brought to the household showcased the beauty of providing love and care in the twilight years, proving that every dog deserves a chance at happiness. His passing gave the family much comfort knowing Jake found a loving home before his time.

10. *Empathy and Advocacy:* Inspired by their rescue dog, Daisy, Mark and Jessica became advocates for animal welfare. Daisy's story motivated them to raise awareness, volunteer at shelters, and work towards creating a community where every dog finds a loving home. They have been involved with the dog rescue movement for over 20 years and raised over 20 million dollars for rescues.

11. *Nightmare to Tranquility:* Bodhi adopted Odi after the passing of his first dog. Odi was set to be euthanized due to his aggressive behavior towards humans after being severely abused and neglected. Bodhi saw something different in his eyes and adopted him immediately. After many years of developing trust and love, Odi is the sweetest and most loving companion any dog lover could embrace. They have been together for 10 years.

12. *Neglected from Love:* Lacie was found online about 4 hours away from Dale. He wanted a puppy as the website portrayed, but when he got there the next day, he found out the website had not been updated and Lacie was almost a year old and only used 3 legs. She had sat in a cage so much one of legs never developed properly. Dale made the decision to rescue her anyway. Dale was a therapist who used his knowledge to heal Lacie back to health both mentally and physically. After several months, Lacie was able to use all 4 legs, jump on the bed, and run with other dogs.

She lived to be 16 and was so well mannered and sweet from the day she left the shelter to her last breath nose to nose with Dale.

Overcoming Obstacles: Rescued Dogs Making a Difference in Society

Rescue dogs are heroes in their own right, tirelessly overcoming obstacles and making a significant impact on society. The stories of these remarkable canines shed light on their struggles, triumphs, and the ways in which they are changing lives. All walks of life can benefit from understanding and supporting the cause of saving rescue dogs in America.

Rescue dogs often come from difficult backgrounds, having endured neglect, abuse, or abandonment. However, their resilience knows no bounds as they overcome these obstacles and emerge as shining examples of determination and love. These dogs teach us valuable lessons in resilience, forgiveness, and the power of second chances. By opening their hearts and homes to rescue dogs, pet owners provide them with the love, care, and stability they need to recover from past traumas. These pet owners are not only rewarded with loyal and affectionate companions but also contribute to a larger movement of creating a more compassionate society.

Society benefits immensely from the presence of rescue dogs. These dogs often go on to become therapy animals, providing comfort and healing to individuals suffering from physical or emotional challenges. Whether it's visiting hospitals, nursing homes, or schools, these four-legged heroes bring smiles to faces and hope to hearts. Furthermore, they serve as ambassadors for adoption and responsible pet ownership, inspiring others to consider rescuing a dog instead of purchasing one from breeders or pet stores.

Therapy dogs are extraordinary canine companions trained to provide comfort, support, and emotional assistance to individuals in various settings. These remarkable animals play a crucial role in therapeutic interventions, offering a unique form of solace and companionship. Their gentle demeanor and natural affinity for human interaction make therapy dogs particularly well-suited for their role. Whether visiting hospitals, nursing homes, schools, or disaster-stricken areas, these dogs have an innate ability to uplift spirits and bring joy to those in need.

The training regimen for therapy dogs includes exposure to a myriad of environments and situations, ensuring they remain calm and focused during their interactions. Their presence has been proven to reduce stress, anxiety, and feelings of loneliness, promoting emotional well-being among those they visit. In educational settings, therapy dogs can aid in literacy programs, providing non-judgmental companionship to struggling readers.

Moreover, therapy dogs contribute to rehabilitation efforts, assisting individuals in physical therapy and offering emotional support in mental health settings. Their impact extends beyond individual therapy sessions, fostering a sense of community and connection. The bond formed between therapy dogs and those they assist is profound, and the unconditional love they provide becomes a catalyst for healing and positive transformation. As the demand for therapy dogs continues to grow, their role in promoting mental and emotional health remains indispensable, showcasing the extraordinary impact that the human-animal bond can have on the well-being of individuals across diverse circumstances and environments.

Recognizing the significance of rescue dogs, government agencies and policymakers have started implementing measures to protect and promote their welfare. Improved legislation and regulations ensure that rescue dogs receive the necessary care, medical attention, and socialization they need while waiting for their forever homes. These initiatives also prioritize educating the public about the importance of adopting rather than purchasing pets, reducing the number of animals in shelters, and combating the cruel cycle of breeding for profit.

Rescue dogs are not just animals in need; they are invaluable members of our society. Through their resilience, love, and unwavering spirit, they teach us about compassion, second chances, and the power of making a difference. By supporting the cause of saving rescue dogs in America, society can contribute to building a more humane and compassionate society for all creatures.

Chapter 8: Building a Brighter Future for Rescue Dogs in America

Encouraging Responsible Breeding Practices

In the quest to save rescue dogs in America, one crucial aspect that cannot be overlooked is the need to encourage responsible breeding practices. The conscious practice of responsible breeding will produce a positive impact on the rescue dog population, and how these improvements can collectively contribute to this cause.

Responsible breeding practices are vital to ensure the well-being of dogs and prevent the overpopulation of rescue dogs. Irresponsible breeding often leads to health issues in dogs due to genetic disorders, poor living conditions, and inadequate veterinary care. These dogs are more likely to end up in shelters or rescue organizations, adding to the already overwhelming number of abandoned or neglected animals.

Pet owners can play a role in promoting responsible breeding practices. By choosing to adopt a rescue dog instead of purchasing one from a breeder, they can help reduce the demand for puppies from irresponsible breeders. Educating themselves about the importance of responsible breeding and the ethical considerations involved will empower pet owners to make informed decisions and contribute to the cause of saving rescue dogs.

Society can also make a significant impact. Promoting awareness campaigns about the benefits of adopting rescue dogs, the consequences of irresponsible breeding, and the rewards of responsible pet ownership can help shift public perception. Encouraging individuals to spay and neuter their pets can also help combat the issue of overpopulation. Additionally, supporting local rescue organizations through donations, volunteering, or fostering can directly contribute to the rescue and rehabilitation of dogs in need.

Encouraging responsible breeding practices allows government agencies to enforce laws that protect against irresponsible methods. Implementing and enforcing stricter regulations and licensing requirements for breeders can help identify irresponsible breeders who prioritize profits over the well-being of animals. Funding programs that promote spaying and neutering, as well as providing financial support to rescue organizations, can also alleviate the burden on these organizations and enable them to save more lives.

Encouraging responsible breeding practices is a crucial step towards saving rescue dogs in America. By educating pet owners about the benefits of adoption, raising awareness in society, and implementing effective government policies, we can collectively make a difference. Nothing is more humane than providing a brighter future for rescue dogs, giving them the love, care, and forever homes they deserve.

Strengthening Adoption Processes and Screening

Strengthening adoption processes and screening measures is a pivotal step in ensuring the well-being of both animals and adoptive families. These enhanced procedures go beyond the conventional adoption checklist, aiming to create a more thorough and tailored approach. Initial screenings involve detailed interviews and questionnaires, searching into the prospective adopter's lifestyle, living situation, and level of commitment. This process helps match the right pet with the right family, considering factors such as energy levels, space, and the adopter's experience with pet ownership. Home visits provide an opportunity to assess the living environment, ensuring it is safe and suitable for the specific needs of the pet. Comprehensive background checks may be conducted to verify an adopter's history of responsible pet ownership and identify any potential red flags.

Education plays a key role in the adoption process. Prospective adopters are provided with resources on pet care, behavioral training, and the long-term responsibilities of pet ownership. By fostering informed decision-making, these educational components contribute to successful, lifelong adoptions. Veterinary references and spaying/neutering commitments are often integral components of the screening process, reinforcing the importance of ongoing health care and population control.

While these stringent measures may seem rigorous, they are designed to ensure that the adoptive family is well-prepared for the responsibilities of pet ownership and that the adopted pet finds a forever home. Strengthening adoption processes not only safeguards the welfare of animals but also helps reduce the likelihood of pets returning to shelters. By prioritizing thorough screenings, adoption agencies and shelters contribute to building lasting, loving connections between pets and their adoptive families, creating environments where both animals and humans can thrive together.

Adopting a rescue dog is a noble act, but it comes with responsibility. It is our duty as pet owners to ensure that we are providing a safe and loving home for these innocent animals who have often experienced neglect, abuse, or abandonment. This is where the adoption process and screening play a pivotal role.

The community plays a critical role in supporting and encouraging the adoption of rescue dogs by raising awareness about the benefits of adopting shelter dogs and dispelling common misconceptions. We can help create a more positive perception of adopting over purchasing pets. Stricter regulations and standards for animal shelters and rescue organizations have provided oversight to help control misleading groups. This will ensure that the screening process is thorough and comprehensive, prioritizing the welfare of the rescue dogs.

Government agencies can help by implementing and enforcing regulations that promote responsible pet ownership, the government can contribute to reducing the number of homeless and abandoned animals. This can be achieved through measures such as mandatory spaying or neutering, promoting micro-chipping, and providing financial assistance or tax incentives for adopting rescue dogs.

A robust adoption process should include a comprehensive screening of potential adopters. This screening process must assess the adopter's ability to provide a safe and suitable environment for the rescue dog. It should involve a thorough background check, including references from veterinarians or previous pet ownership experiences. Potential adopters should be required to participate in education and training programs, ensuring they are knowledgeable about the specific needs and challenges that rescue dogs may face. By strengthening adoption processes and screening, we can ensure that rescue dogs find loving forever homes and are spared from further trauma or neglect. This not only benefits the individual dogs but also contributes to the overall well-being of our society and promotes responsible pet ownership.

The importance of strengthening adoption processes and screening in the context of saving rescue dogs must become a priority for dog lovers. By actively involving pet owners, society, and the government in this process, we can create a society that prioritizes the welfare of these voiceless animals, providing them with the second chance they truly deserve.

Continuing Education and Support for Rescue Dog Owners

Rescuing a dog is a noble act that not only saves a life but also brings immeasurable joy and companionship. However, it's important to recognize that rescue dogs often come with unique challenges that require ongoing education and support for their owners. Continued education provides valuable resources for rescue dog owners to ensure a successful and fulfilling relationship with their furry companions.

One of the primary reasons why continuing education is crucial for rescue dog owners is to better understand the background and history of their canine companions. Many rescue dogs have experienced trauma or neglect, which can manifest in behavioral issues. By learning about the specific needs and triggers of rescue dogs, owners can provide the necessary support and create a safe and loving environment.

Ongoing education allows owners to stay up to date with the latest training techniques and behavioral interventions. Rescued dogs often require specialized training to overcome any fear or anxiety they may have developed. By arming themselves with knowledge, owners can effectively address these challenges and help their dogs lead happy and well-adjusted lives.

Support networks are also essential for rescue dog owners. Connecting with other pet owners who have rescued dogs can offer a sense of community and shared experiences. Local rescue organizations and animal shelters often provide support groups, training classes, and workshops tailored specifically for rescue dog owners. These resources offer a safe space to discuss challenges, seek advice, and share successes, creating a network of support that is invaluable in the journey of rescuing and rehabilitating dogs.

In addition to local resources, online platforms and forums dedicated to rescue dog owners can be an excellent source of information and support. These platforms connect owners with experts, trainers, and fellow pet lovers, allowing for continuous learning and growth. By actively engaging in these communities, owners can access a wealth of knowledge and seek guidance whenever needed.

Finally, it's crucial for society and government to recognize the importance of continuing education and support for rescue dog owners. By investing in educational programs and resources, we can empower owners to provide the best care for their rescue dogs. Additionally, government initiatives can help increase awareness and promote responsible ownership, ultimately reducing the number of dogs in shelters and ensuring more successful adoptions.

Continuing education and support for rescue dog owners are essential components of advocating for rescue dogs. By equipping owners with knowledge and resources, we can create a society that understands and empathizes with the unique challenges faced by rescue dogs. Together, let us champion the cause of rescue dogs and provide them with the love, care, and support they deserve.

Conclusion: Uniting for the Voiceless

In the journey towards advocating for rescue dogs in America, it becomes clear that the responsibility lies not only with pet owners, but also with society and the government. The collective effort of these three key stakeholders is crucial in bringing about a positive change for the voiceless beings who rely on our compassion and action. This book is a call to action, urging pet owners, society, and the government to unite in their efforts to save rescue dogs in America.

Pet owners, you hold a unique power in your hands. By adopting a rescue dog, you are not only giving a deserving animal a second chance at life but also setting an example for others to follow. Your love and care can transform the life of a rescue dog and provide them with the happiness they deserve. Embrace responsible pet ownership by spaying/neutering your pets, providing proper training, and ensuring they receive regular veterinary care. Educate yourself and others about the benefits of rescue dogs, their potential, and their ability to bring joy to any home.

Society, it is time to recognize the immense value that rescue dogs bring to our communities. They are more than just abandoned animals; they possess endless potential as loyal companions, therapy dogs, and working partners. Support local animal rescue organizations by volunteering your time, donating resources, or spreading awareness through social media. Encourage businesses to adopt rescue dogs as office pets, promoting a compassionate work environment. By shifting societal attitudes towards rescue dogs, we can create a society that values their lives and ensures their well-being.

Government, it is imperative that you implement policies and regulations that protect the rights and welfare of rescue dogs. Allocate funding for shelters and rescue organizations to provide proper care, rehabilitation, and adoption programs. Enforce strict laws against animal abuse and neglect, ensuring that those who mistreat animals face severe consequences. Develop educational campaigns that promote responsible pet ownership, reaching out to schools, communities, and the media. By prioritizing the well-being of rescue dogs, you will be sending a powerful message that animal rights matter and are a fundamental aspect of a compassionate society.

The crisis of rescue dogs in America demands action from pet owners, society, and the government. By coming together and uniting for the voiceless, we can create a future where no rescue dog is left behind. Let us remember that the love and care we give to these animals will be repaid tenfold in the form of unwavering loyalty, boundless affection, and a lifelong companionship that will enrich our lives. Through a collective effort, we can create a eutopia of bliss for rescue dogs in America.

Acknowledgments

I would like to take this opportunity to express my deepest gratitude and appreciation to all those who have played a significant role in the creation and success of this book, "Saving Dongs in America." This project would not have been possible without the unwavering support and contributions of numerous individuals and organizations.

First and foremost, I would like to extend my heartfelt gratitude to all the rescue dog owners who shared their inspiring stories and experiences with me. Your dedication and love for these incredible animals have been the driving force behind this book. Your stories have shed light on the challenges faced by rescue dogs in America and have served as a powerful reminder of the impact that love and compassion can have on their lives.

I would also like to express my sincere appreciation to the various rescue organizations and shelters across the country. Your tireless efforts in saving and rehabilitating rescue dogs have not only touched the lives of countless animals but have also transformed the communities in which you operate. Your commitment to providing a second chance to these dogs is truly commendable, and I am grateful for the opportunity to shed light on your invaluable work.

To the pet owners who have opened their hearts and homes to rescue dogs, thank you for your compassion and willingness to make a difference. Your decision to adopt a rescue dog not only saves a life but also sets an example for others to follow. Your stories of transformation and the unbreakable bond you share with your four-legged companions serve as a testament to the immense rewards of rescuing.

I would also like to acknowledge the support of society and government in addressing the issues surrounding rescue dogs in America. The collective effort to raise awareness about the importance of adoption, promoting responsible pet ownership, and implementing laws and regulations to protect these vulnerable animals is truly commendable. Your dedication to making a positive change in the lives of rescue dogs is an inspiration to us all.

Finally, I want to express my deepest gratitude to my family and friends for their unwavering support throughout this journey. Your encouragement, understanding, and patience have been invaluable, and I am truly grateful for your presence in my life.

"Saving Dogs in America" is a collaborative effort that would not have been possible without the support of rescue dog owners, organizations, pet owners, society, and government. It is my hope that this book will serve as a call to action and inspire others to join the movement of saving rescue dogs in America. As advocates for rescue dogs in America, it is crucial to have a solid understanding of the issues at hand and the resources available to address them. Please take the time to share your world with a rescue dog. Let your heart be open and your home be a home. This is the way...

References

1. *American Society for the Prevention of Cruelty to Animals (ASPCA):* The ASPCA is one of the leading organizations dedicated to preventing animal cruelty and promoting the welfare of animals. Their website offers a wealth of information on rescue dogs, adoption, and ways to get involved.

2. *The Humane Society of the United States (HSUS):* HSUS is another prominent organization that advocates for animal welfare, including rescue dogs. Their website provides valuable resources on adopting rescue dogs, volunteering at shelters, and legislative efforts to protect animals.

3. *The Shelter Pet Project:* This collaborative effort between the HSUS, the ASPCA, and Maddie's Fund aims to increase pet adoption from shelters. Their website features heartwarming adoption stories, tips for finding the perfect rescue dog, and a comprehensive database of adoptable pets across the country.

4. *Centers for Disease Control and Prevention (CDC):* The CDC offers valuable guidelines on responsible pet ownership, including the proper care and handling of rescue dogs. Their resources help pet owners understand the potential health risks and preventive measures associated with pet ownership.

5. *National Animal Control Association (NACA):* NACA is an organization dedicated to the professional development of animal control officers and the promotion of animal welfare. Their website provides resources on animal control practices, including the rescue and rehabilitation of dogs.

6. *United States Department of Agriculture (USDA):* The USDA plays a vital role in regulating animal welfare, including the standards for

commercial dog breeders and animal transport. Their website provides information on animal welfare laws, inspection reports, and licensing requirements.

7. *Local Animal Shelters and Rescue Organizations:* Each community has its own network of animal shelters and rescue organizations. These local resources are often the first point of contact for pet owners interested in adopting a rescue dog or supporting animal welfare initiatives. Research and reach out to your local shelters to learn about adoption processes, volunteer opportunities, and fundraising events.

By consulting these references, pet owners, society, and the government can gain a deeper understanding of the challenges faced by rescue dogs in America and find ways to contribute to their well-being. Together, we can make a difference and give a voice to the voiceless.

Don't miss out!

Visit the website below and you can sign up to receive emails whenever Randy Woodrum publishes a new book. There's no charge and no obligation.

https://books2read.com/r/B-A-TKUCB-YQXTC

BOOKS 2 READ

Connecting independent readers to independent writers.